People Power
Buying and Selling in the United States

Kevin Adkins

Contents

Rigby

A Harcourt Achieve Imprint

www.Rigby.com

1-800-531-5015

Introduction

Imagine that there's a very good baker named Bernadette who has been working on a new donut recipe. She's spent a long time making sure that the recipe is just right, including adding a little more sugar, a little less flour, and just enough yeast. She's tried many different types of frosting, too, adding a bit more butter every time so it will be light, creamy, and delicious.

Once the recipe is perfect, Bernadette makes a big batch of donuts for her friends and family. Everyone loves them—in fact, they think these are some of the best donuts they've ever tasted!

Bernadette thinks that other people would like her donuts, too, and decides to start a business selling them. There's just one problem: Bernadette doesn't have enough money to open a store. In some countries, that would mean she wouldn't be able to start her business. However, she has a chance to open her donut business in the United States.

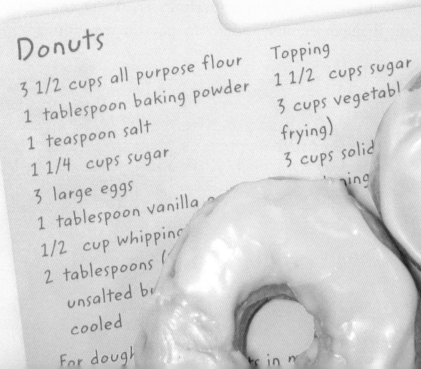

Donuts

3 1/2 cups all purpose flour
1 tablespoon baking powder
1 teaspoon salt
1 1/4 cups sugar
3 large eggs
1 tablespoon vanilla
1/2 cup whippinc
2 tablespoons (
  unsalted b
  cooled
For dough

Topping
1 1/2 cups sugar
3 cups vegetabl
  frying)
3 cups solid
  ning

lend. St
and melted

CHAPTER 1

From Idea to Business

How Much Will It Cost?

Bernadette starts thinking about what she will need to open her store. She has to find a good location with big ovens and a nice display case for her donuts. She'll also need pots and pans, a cash register, and enough flour, sugar, and other ingredients to make a lot of donuts.

After she's done she figures out the cost of each item—these are her expenses, and they add up to a lot of money! However, if she can sell enough donuts every week, she'll make enough money to pay for everything.

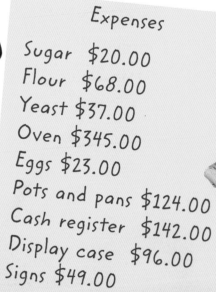

Expenses

Sugar $20.00
Flour $68.00
Yeast $37.00
Oven $345.00
Eggs $23.00
Pots and pans $124.00
Cash register $142.00
Display case $96.00
Signs $49.00

Finding Money

The next day Bernadette goes to the bank, bringing with her two dozen donuts, which she passes out to the people working there. Bernadette then asks if the bank will loan her the money she needs to open her store.

The bank tells Bernadette that even though her donuts are really delicious, they have decided not to give her a loan. She's disappointed, but they tell her not to give up, because there are many other ways to start a business.

Starting a Business

Write a Business Plan

Bernadette writes a list of everything she needs to open her store, how much it will cost, and how many donuts she'll have to sell to pay for everything and still make money. This is called a *business plan*.

Find Investors

Once Bernadette has a business plan, she shows it to people who are interested in her donuts and asks them to give her some money to open her store.

- If people like the plan and believe Bernadette will sell a lot of donuts, they will invest, or lend her money that she will use to open her store. Then Bernadette can sell the donuts and earn more money.

- If people don't like the plan and believe Bernadette won't sell many donuts, they will not invest in her business, and she will have to write a new business plan.

Open Business

Bernadette uses the money from her investors to open her store.

- If people like Bernadette's donuts, she will sell a lot of them, and her business will be a success!

- If people don't like the donuts, Bernadette will not sell enough of them, and she will have to close her store.

Keep Making Donuts!

Bernadette's donuts are selling very quickly, and she has to rush to make more. Her business is doing well!

Pay Investors

Bernadette's business is a success, so she has made a profit, or money left over after expenses are paid. She gives some of the money that she borrowed back to her investors.

Opening Day!

Bernadette opens her store and sells 300 donuts the first day. In fact so many people want to buy her donuts that she has to keep making more. If things keep going this well, she'll have to open a bigger store and hire more people!

As Bernadette closes the store for the night, she thinks about how lucky she is to live in a place where there are so many opportunities. But it wasn't always this way–for the first people who came to the United States, things were very different.

CHAPTER 2

A Mercantile Economy

A System

Who makes the things that we buy? Who decides how many of each one to make and how much money to charge for each? The answers depend on a country's **economy**, which is a system that determines

- what **products** (items or services for sale) will be made;

- who will produce, or make, the products that will be sold;

- who the products are sold to; and

- the price **consumers** (people who buy the products) pay to buy them.

The first people to come to America had an economy, but it was very different from the one we use today.

Mercantilism—Guided by Government

In the 1600s England had an economy based on **mercantilism**. In this system the government decided what products should be made, how many should be made, and how much money people paid for them. England's government wanted to have the most gold and silver, so the people worked hard to set up an economy that would bring a lot of money into the country. England earned money through **exports**, or products sent out of England to be sold and used in another country. England's government didn't like buying many **imports**, or products brought into England from other countries.

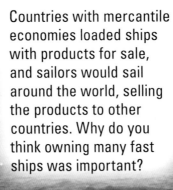

Countries with mercantile economies loaded ships with products for sale, and sailors would sail around the world, selling the products to other countries. Why do you think owning many fast ships was important?

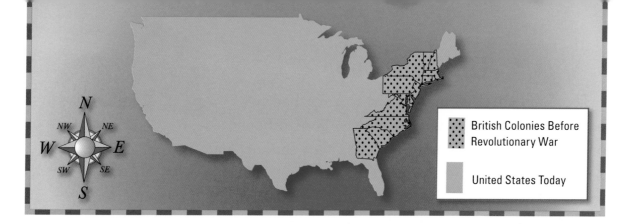

British Colonies Before Revolutionary War

United States Today

Exporting Wealth, Importing Trouble

To make exports England needed **natural resources,** which are useful materials found in nature. European explorers had recently arrived in America and found that it was rich in natural resources such as wood and iron. The English government sent people to live there, and these people, called *colonists*, worked hard to send natural resources back to England. The people in England used these resources to make products–furniture, clothing, and jewelry–that could be exported to other countries and sold there.

In America the colonists grew most of their own food and made most of their own clothes. However, the colonists had to buy some things from people in other countries because some products couldn't be found in America. For example, the colonists had to import sugar from other countries. Colonists could buy sugar from England, but it was very expensive, so most colonists bought less expensive sugar from Spain or France.

Unfair Taxes

The English government wasn't very happy about the colonists buying products from other countries. The government added a **tax** (money paid to the government) to the price of products that the colonists imported from countries other than England. These taxes made French and Spanish sugar so expensive that the colonists couldn't afford to buy it. That was great for the English government—now the colonists would have to buy sugar from England!

Looking for a Change

Soon the colonists were paying many different taxes to England, and after a while, they became very unhappy. "It isn't fair," the colonists said, "that we have to pay English taxes when we don't even live in England!" Some colonists thought that they shouldn't have to follow England's rules anymore. They also wondered if there was a better kind of economy than mercantilism—but what other type of system was there?

A man in Scotland thought he had the answer.

In 1773 the colonists protested a tax on tea by dumping imported British tea into the ocean. This was later called the *Boston Tea Party*.

13

CHAPTER 3

New Ideas, New Country

A Declaration and an Important Book

In 1776 a Scottish man named Adam Smith wrote *The Wealth of Nations*, a book about a new type of economy. That same year American colonists wrote the Declaration of Independence, which stated that no longer would the colonists follow England's rules.

Many of the people who wrote the Declaration of Independence read Smith's book and liked what it said—the book influenced the future of America.

A Different Opinion

Adam Smith thought that mercantilism was a bad idea. Smith wrote in his book that governments should do things like make laws and keep the country safe from danger, but he argued that governments shouldn't make decisions about the economy. He wrote that a country's wealth was based on making products that people wanted to buy, not just on how much money the country had collected. Smith also believed that a country would be wealthier if it could export and import products without paying high taxes.

Adam Smith

Laissez-faire

People like Adam Smith believed that governments should follow a plan called *laissez-faire*, a French term that means "allow to do." A government that follows this plan does not decide how the economy works—the people who live in that country decide.

Capitalism—People Power

In 1776 the colonists were in the middle of the American Revolution, a war between England and the American colonies. The colonists were fighting to be free from England's rules, and in 1783 the colonists won the American Revolution and formed their own country, the United States. They could create whatever economy was best for them, and they decided that the ideas in Smith's book might be the economy they wanted.

A New System

The ideas in Smith's book were the beginning of **free enterprise**—an economy where the people are free to decide what products to make, where to make them, how much to sell them for, and who to sell them to. It is called *free enterprise* because people are free to make decisions without help from the government. Sometimes free enterprise is also called *capitalism.*

A free enterprise system allows people like Bernadette to take an idea and turn it into a product that everyone can enjoy. Free enterprise also helps Bernadette figure out what products to make based on what items people want to buy.

CHAPTER 4

Supply and Demand

How Much to Make?

Bernadette knows that her donuts are delicious, but she also wants them to look good, so she adds colored sprinkles to some donuts and she spreads others with pink frosting. But how will she know how many of each kind of donut to make?

Imagine it's Saturday morning, and your parents take you to Bernadette's donut store for a treat. Her donuts look so good that you can almost taste them already, and they come in two different kinds: sprinkled donuts and pink-frosted donuts.

Making Choices

Your mom or dad asks you what kind of donut you want. For some reason you think that the pink-frosted donuts look even more delicious than the ones with sprinkles—and you're not the only one who thinks so. Most people who come into the store want pink-frosted donuts, which means that the **demand** (how much people want to buy something) for pink-frosted donuts is very high.

Just Enough of Everything

When you are in the store, Bernadette has 15 sprinkled donuts for sale and 20 customers who want sprinkled donuts. That means that the **supply** (products available for sale) almost meets the demand—she has almost enough for everybody who wants to buy one.

However, there are 40 people who want a pink-frosted donut, and only 20 of them for sale. The supply of frosted donuts is much lower than the demand.

Will Bernadette make more pink-frosted or sprinkled donuts? She'll probably increase her supply of frosted donuts because there is a higher demand for them.

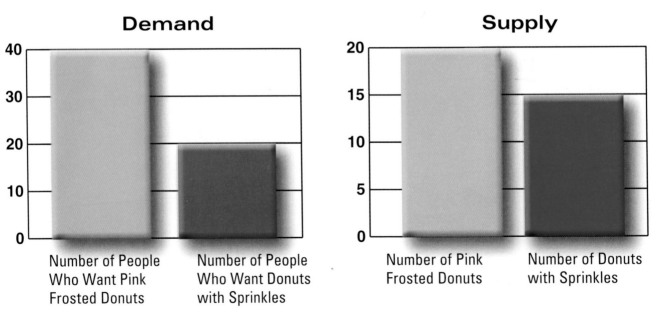

How Much to Pay?

Of course if there aren't enough pink-frosted donuts for everyone who wants one, people might be willing to pay more for them, and Bernadette can make more money by raising the price. If the price is too high, her customers could decide to buy a sprinkled donut instead—or nothing at all. Understanding supply and demand helps businesses make just enough of a product and sell it for the right prices.

Supply and Demand

Why would Bernadette have a sale with a discounted price for her donuts with sprinkles?

Sprinkled Donuts now 30% off!

The Right Price for the Right Product

Bernadette decides to sell the pink-frosted donuts for 50 cents and to sell the sprinkled donuts for only 40 cents. Since frosted donuts are so popular, people are happy to pay a little extra, and Bernadette sells them all. Since the sprinkled donuts are cheaper than the pink-frosted donuts, some people decide to buy them instead, and Bernadette also sells all of the sprinkled donuts.

Luckily, Bernadette has one pink-frosted donut left for you—and it tastes just as sweet and delicious as you thought it would!

You're enjoying a pink-frosted donut, other people saved some money by buying sprinkled donuts, and Bernadette's store is doing great. You're probably thinking that a free enterprise economy works very well–and you're right! But every system has its problems.

CHAPTER 5

Bigger Is Not Always Better

Another Choice

Imagine that there's a very big company, Donut Giant, that has been making donuts for many years. There is a Donut Giant store down the street from Bernadette's store, and they make hundreds of donuts every morning—many more than Bernadette can make. They also know how popular Bernadette's pink-frosted donuts are, so they've started making some frosted donuts in addition to sprinkled.

The next weekend you are walking to Bernadette's donut shop, thinking about how much you're going to enjoy eating a donut. As you pass Donut Giant, you notice a sign in the window that reads: "Sale! Frosted donuts only 35 cents!"

Frosted donuts
only 35 cents!

Staying Even

At Bernadette's store, you look across the street and see Bernadette putting a sign in her window that reads: "Frosted donuts now only 39 cents!" Bernadette knows that if Donut Giant is selling donuts for a lower price, people might go to Donut Giant instead of her store, so she decided to lower the price of her donuts as well.

Of course, once Donut Giant sees Bernadette's sign, they might decide to make the price of frosted donuts even lower. And if that happens, Bernadette might be in trouble, because she can't afford to lower prices again.

Adding Up Costs

Bernadette has to pay for the materials she uses to make her donuts—ingredients like flour, sugar, and yeast. She also has to pay her electricity and gas bills, and the rent for her store. After she's paid all of her expenses, she can determine that it costs 15 cents to make each donut. Bernadette needs to make enough money to pay her expenses, pay her investors, and have some money left over for herself. She needs to make a profit, or sell her donuts for more money than she spent to make them, so she has to charge at least 39 cents.

Donut Giant buys materials from the same supply company that Bernadette does. So they must pay the same price that she does, right?

Price Wars

Expenses vs. Price

	Bernadette's Donuts	Donut Giant's Donuts
Cost to make one donut	$0.15	$0.10
Price of donut	$0.39	$0.35
Profit	$0.24	$0.25

Bigger Business, Smaller Prices

Since they make thousands of donuts, Donut Giant probably pays less for the ingredients. Donut Giant buys so much flour, yeast, and sugar that the supply company agrees to sell materials to them for less money than it would to someone like Bernadette, who only buys a small amount of materials. Donut Giant can make a donut for only 10 cents, which means they can sell it for a little less than Bernadette and still make a profit.

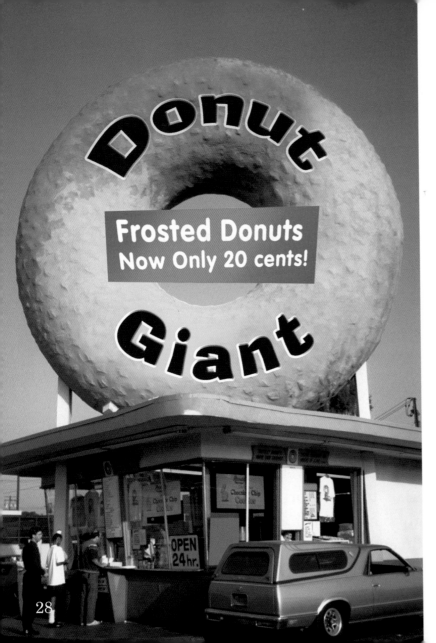

Frosted Donuts Now Only 20 cents!

Donut Giant may sell its donuts for less money, but Bernadette's donuts taste better, so people don't mind paying more money for them. In fact, a lot of Donut Giant's customers have started buying their donuts at Bernadette's store instead of at Donut Giant.

Donut Giant may not be very happy that people are buying donuts from Bernadette and not from them. What can they do to get people to come back to their store? They may decide that if the price of their donuts were even lower, people would come back to Donut Giant. They start selling donuts for only 20 cents. Does that sound fair to you?

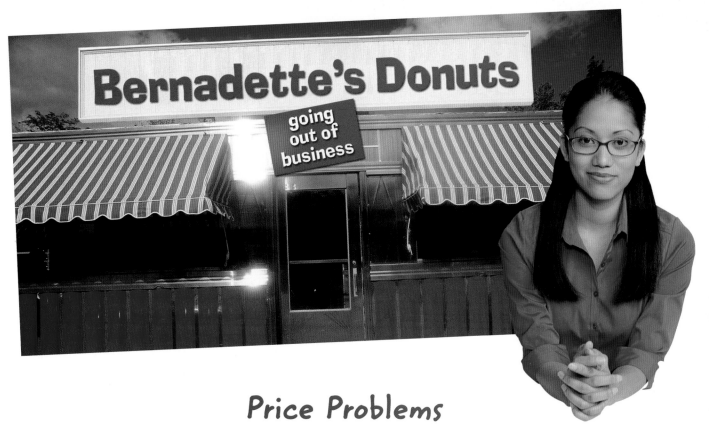

Price Problems

Bernadette can't lower the price of her donuts. She hasn't been in business for very long and has very little money in the bank, so she can't afford to sell her donuts for less than what they cost to make. If people decided to buy Donut Giant's less expensive donuts, Bernadette wouldn't sell enough donuts, and she would run out of money and be forced to close her store.

Monopoly

If Donut Giant decides to keep selling donuts at the lower price until all the small donut stores like Bernadette's run out of money and close, Donut Giant will be the only store in the area where people can buy donuts. Donut Giant will be a **monopoly**, which is a company or a group of companies working together that controls the supply of a certain product. If Donut Giant is a monopoly, it's the only store that supplies donuts, and it can charge as much as it wants for its donuts!

That doesn't sound very fair, does it? The United States government doesn't think monopolies are fair either.

CHAPTER 6

Keeping Things Fair

Competition

For a successful free enterprise system, there has to be **competition**, or different companies that make and sell similar products. Competition helps keep prices fair because people have a choice of where to buy the products they want. If a company charges too much for its product, people will be able to buy a similar product from someone else for less money.

Think about the American colonists. They had to buy all of their sugar from England, and England charged them way too much money—even though Spain and France were selling sugar for much less! This was a kind of monopoly, and it caused a lot of problems. That's why the U.S. government has laws that keep companies from getting too big today.

The Government's Role

In a free enterprise system, the people decide for themselves how the economy will work, so you might be wondering why the government is involved in the economy at all. The people were responsible for all of the decisions on the economy at first. However, after a while there were problems with how people used the free enterprise system, and the government decided to step in.

Anti-monopoly Laws

In the late 1800s some companies joined together to control prices and production, which prevented competition. In 1890 the U.S. government passed the Sherman Act. This law allows the government to divide monopolies into smaller companies that compete with each other.

Over the years more laws were passed including the Clayton Act, which makes it illegal for a company like Donut Giant to lower prices so much that smaller companies go out of business.

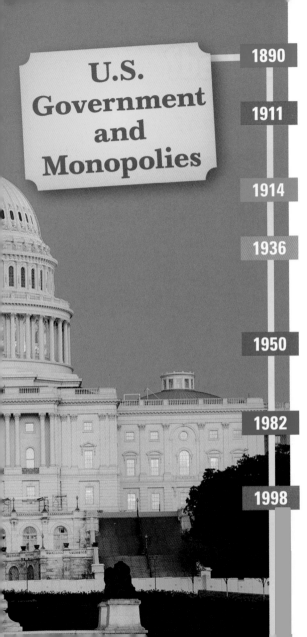

U.S. Government and Monopolies

1890 — **The Sherman Act**—Groups of companies are banned from working together to control trade.

1911 — **Breakup of Standard Oil**—The U.S. government uses the Sherman Act to separate Standard Oil Company into more than 30 competing businesses.

1914 — **Clayton Act**—Companies are not allowed to lower prices to close down other businesses.

1936 — **Robinson-Portman Act**—Small stores are protected from larger chain stores forcing them out of business by selling products for prices that are lower than normal.

1950 — **Celler-Kefauver Act**—Limits are set for companies that want to join together to make one larger company that would reduce competition.

1982 — **Breakup of AT&T**—The U.S. government breaks the phone company AT&T into seven phone companies that were smaller.

1998 — **Government vs. Microsoft**—The U.S. government sues Microsoft Corporation for violating anti-monopoly laws with its computer operating system company.

CHAPTER 7

Monopolies—Good or Bad?

New Rules, New Problems

Today two agencies in the U.S. government, the Federal Trade Commission (FTC) and the Antitrust Division, work to make sure that companies don't become monopolies.

Some people think that the government doesn't do enough to keep companies from becoming monopolies—or from working together like a monopoly. Others think that the government does too much, and that taking big companies to court is actually hurting the economy.

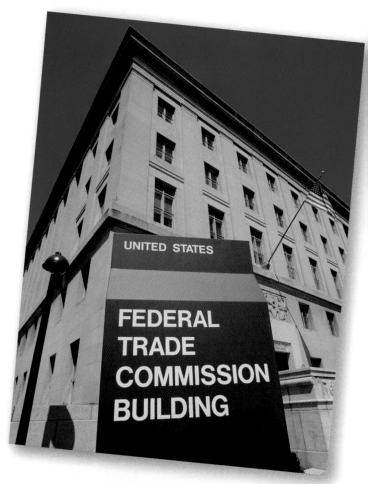

UNITED STATES

FEDERAL TRADE COMMISSION BUILDING

Some Monopolies Are Good

Why would some people think that breaking up monopolies is a bad idea? Donut Giant is so big that it doesn't have to pay as much for its ingredients, which means it can sell its donuts for a lower price and still make a profit. That means customers can buy cheaper donuts! Shouldn't Donut Giant be allowed to give people the products that they want at low prices?

Too Many Phone Companies

People who believe that some monopolies are good for the economy might say that dividing companies is a big mistake. Before 1982 AT&T was the only phone company in the United States. This meant that whether you were calling across the street or across the country, you used the same company, and the charges for all calls went on the same bill.

After the government broke AT&T into smaller companies, people received bills from two companies—one for local calls (calls within the city where you live) and one for long-distance calls (calls across the state or the country). This made making a phone call more difficult and sometimes even more expensive, and that's not good, is it?

All Monopolies Are Bad

Other people say that the government has to break up monopolies so that people will keep making new products. For example, Bernadette worked very hard to make her donuts as delicious as possible, and she succeeded. But if she knew that Donut Giant was a monopoly and would make her go out of business, she probably wouldn't have opened a store in the first place.

Computer Control

Some people argue that monopolies don't give people like Bernadette a chance to start businesses. Some people accused Microsoft Corporation and their computer software business of limiting competition. Microsoft had made deals with many of the companies that make computers. The computer companies would always use Microsoft's software programs in the computers that they made, even if someone else made a similar program.

The government said that these deals kept consumers from having a choice of which programs they could use. After a long trial the government and Microsoft agreed on a plan to change how Microsoft does business.

Should the government divide big companies so smaller ones like Bernadette's can have a chance at becoming successful businesses? Or should the government not have a role in the economy and let the people make all the decisions? What do you think?

Glossary

free enterprise an economy in which the people decide what to make and what to buy; also called *capitalism*

competition when more than one company makes a product or provides a service

consumers people who buy products

demand how much consumers want to buy a product

economy a system that determines what products are made, who makes them, and how much they cost to buy

export a product that is sold to another country

import a product that is bought from another country

mercantilism an economic system in which a country's government decides what products are made, who makes them, and how much they cost to buy

monopoly a company that is the only supplier of a product; a company that has no competition

natural resources materials found in nature that can be turned into products

products items or services for sale

supply the amount of a product that is available for consumers to buy

tax money added to the price of a product by the government

Index